MW00720760

Chefs' Special

Thai Kitchen

Thai Kitchen

Compiled by Master Chefs of India

Lustre Press
Roli Books

Flavours of Thailand

Thailand is a beautiful and fertile country which produces some of the best food in the world. For a place which cultivates the rice crop and is watered by myriad waterways, developing a highly sophisticated cuisine based primarily on rice and fish has been a logical progression. Trade with the East Indies brought cloves and nutmeg to ancient Thailand, while the pungent chilli pepper came from South America. Thai food soon came to be identified with seasonings, both hot and subtle. There are clean citrus tastes from kaffir limes, lime leaves, lemon grass, sour tamarind; a sweet touch from coconut milk; a distinctive ginger-garlic flavour, that of galangal and *krachai*; and the all-pervading chilly dominance. These are skilfully blended in each dish so that no one flavour is overpowering and there is a balance between hot, sour, sweet and salty. This results in a remarkably fresh, clean and exciting taste that is distinctively Thai.

Thai shrimp paste made with condiments like salt, pepper, ginger, cinnamon, cloves, garlic, white onions, nutmeg and several strongly flavoured herbs gives Thai food its unique character. Rice noodles, meat or fish curries in coconut milk, crisp salads (*yam*), soups (*tom yum*), a spicy hot dipping sauce (*nam prig*) comprise a typical Thai meal.

The Thai diet is a very healthy one — plenty of fresh vegetables and fruits, good quality rice, noodles and small amounts of meat and fish. Dairy products are not widely consumed by the majority of Thai people and cattle-rearing is done on a small scale due to the climate and topography of Thailand. Pigs, chicken and ducks are more commonly found here and this is reflected in the recipes.

Fish is very important in the Thai diet. Most often the fish is dried, salted or turned into fish paste or fish sauce. It is highly nutritious, providing a good quality of essential proteins.

A Thai meal generally consists of different dishes, plus a large bowl of rice. There might be a soup — served either in a large bowl which everyone can dip into or in small individual bowls, a curry, a steamed or fried vegetarian or non-vegetarian dish, a salad, noodles, various sauces and pickles. Fresh fruits add the finishing touch to the meal. All the dishes are served simultaneously and they are placed around one large central bowl containing rice. It is not Thai practice to put everything on one's plate at once and eat all the preparations together. The Thai like to savour all the different tastes and textures separately.

The recipes in this book are very quick and simple to prepare. Not only are they tasty, they cater to those who are health conscious as the food is cooked quickly and lightly so as to preserve the maximum nutrients.

Thai cuisine is a pleasure to cook. Crisp, tangy, nutritious, delicious, spicy and wholesome — take 100 gm of adventurous spirit, deep-fry in 10 tbsp of enthusiasm, season with a pinch of experimentation and create your own Thai gourmet delight!

◀ *Green Curry Paste*

Red Curry Paste ▶

Basic Thai Pastes

Green Curry Paste (makes ½ cup)
Ingredients: 15 green chillies; 45 gm shallots, chopped; 15 gm garlic, chopped; 15 gm galangal, chopped; 3 gm kaffir lime rind, chopped; 5 gm coriander root, chopped; 5 black peppercorns; 15 gm coriander seeds; 5 gm cumin seeds; 5 gm salt; 5 gm shrimp paste.

Method: Dry roast the coriander and cumin seeds for 5 minutes. Cool, grind to a powder and keep aside. Blend the remaining ingredients together (except the shrimp paste). Add the coriander-cumin seed mixture and the shrimp paste; blend further into a fine paste. Store refrigerated and use as required.

Red Curry Paste (makes ¾ cup)
Ingredients: 13 red chillies, small, dried; 45 gm shallots, chopped; 60 gm garlic, chopped; 15 gm galangal, chopped; 30 gm lemon grass, chopped; 10 gm kaffir lime rind; 15 gm coriander root, chopped; 20 black peppercorns; 5 gm shrimp paste; 15 gm coriander seeds; 5 gm cumin seeds.

Method: Dry roast the coriander and cumin seeds for 5 minutes. Cool, grind to a powder and keep aside. Blend the remaining ingredients together (except the shrimp paste). Add the coriander-cumin seed mixture and the shrimp paste; blend into a fine paste. Store refrigerated and use as required.

◄ Yellow Curry Paste

Massamaman Curry Paste ▶

Yellow Curry Paste (makes ½ cup)

Ingredients: 3 red chillies, dried; 45 gm shallots, chopped; 15 gm garlic, chopped; 15 gm ginger, chopped; 5 gm coriander seeds; 5 gm cumin seeds; 15 gm lemon grass, chopped; 5 gm shrimp paste; 10 gm curry powder.

Method: Deseed the chillies, soak in hot water for 15 minutes. Heat a wok; add the shallots, garlic, ginger, coriander and cumin seeds. Dry roast for a few minutes. Allow to cool and then grind to a powder. Blend the remaining ingredients. Add the shallots, garlic, ginger, coriander and cumin seed mixture and blend further to obtain a fine-textured paste. Store refrigerated and use as required.

Massaman Curry Paste (makes ½ cup)

Ingredients: 3 red chillies, dried; 45 gm shallots, chopped; 30 gm garlic, chopped; 5 gm galangal, chopped; 30 gm lemon grass, chopped; 2 cloves; 5 gm coriander seeds; 5 gm cumin seeds; 5 black peppercorns; 5 gm shrimp paste; 5 gm salt.

Method: Deseed the chillies, soak in hot water for 15 minutes. Heat a wok; add the shallots, garlic, galangal, lemon grass, cloves, coriander and cumin seeds. Dry roast for 5 minutes. Allow to cool and grind to a powder. Blend the remaining ingredients except shrimp paste. Add the shallots, garlic, galangal, lemon grass, cloves, coriander mixture with the shrimp paste; blend to get a paste. Store refrigerated and use as required.

Tom Yam Koong

Traditional Thai soup with prawns

Preparation time: 15 min.
Cooking time: 10 min.
Serves: 2-4

Ingredients:

Prawn stock	4 cups / 800 ml
Mushrooms, sliced	150 gm
Lemon grass, chopped	80 gm
Lemon leaves, chopped	6
Red chillies, chopped	4
Kha, sliced	80 gm
Prawns, cleaned	150 gm
Fish sauce	2 tbsp / 30 ml
Chilli paste	2 tbsp / 30 gm
Tamarind extract	3 tbsp / 45 ml
Lemon juice	4 tbsp / 60 ml

Method:

1. Heat the prawn stock in a pan; add the vegetables, prawns, fish sauce, chilli paste, tamarind extract and lemon juice.
2. Let it simmer for 5-10 minutes or until the vegetables are tender. Remove from the heat.
3. Transfer to a soup bowl and serve hot.

Kaeng Jued Woon Sen Koong
Chicken and prawn soup with vermicelli

Preparation time: 15 min.
Cooking time: 20 min.
Serves: 2-4

Ingredients:

Vermicelli	240 gm
Chicken, minced	240 gm
Chicken stock	4 cups / 800 ml
Prawns, cleaned	80 gm
Mushrooms, chopped	80 gm
Fish sauce to taste	
White pepper powder	a pinch or two
Celery, chopped	80 gm
Garlic, chopped	20 gm
Spring onions, chopped	40 gm
Green coriander	4-8 sprigs

Method:

1. Soak the vermicelli in sufficient water. Drain and keep aside.
2. Divide the chicken mince into equal portions and shape into balls.
3. Heat the chicken stock in a wok; add the chicken balls and prawns. Bring to a boil.
4. Add the mushrooms, fish sauce and white pepper powder. Simmer for 15-20 minutes.
5. In a soup bowl, place the vermicelli along with the celery, garlic and spring onions.
6. Pour the prepared soup on top and serve hot, garnished with green coriander.

Tom Jieu Hoi
Mussel soup

Preparation time: 20 min.
Cooking time: 20 min.
Serves: 2-4

Ingredients:

Mussels, washed, soaked for
   1 hour in cold water   500 gm
Coconut milk   1½ cups / 300 ml
Fish stock   3 cups / 600 ml
Rice vermicelli, soaked for
   15-20 minutes   5 tbsp / 75 gm
Ginger, finely chopped   1 tbsp / 15 gm
Lemon grass, chopped   ½ stalk
Fish sauce   1 tbsp / 15 ml
Lime juice   1 tbsp / 15 ml
Green coriander to garnish

Method:

1. Remove the beards of the mussels. Drain and tap any open shells to ensure they close.
2. Cook the mussels covered over moderate heat, in a saucepan for 3-4 minutes. The mussels will open and release their liquid. Those that do not open should be thrown away. Remove the mussels with a slotted spoon and keep aside.
3. Add the remaining ingredients and simmer for 15 minutes. Add the mussels and simmer for another minute.
4. Serve garnished with green coriander.

Tom Jieu Moo Sup Nomai

Pork and bamboo shoot soup

Preparation time: 8 min.
Cooking time: 10 min.
Serves: 2-4

Ingredients:

Chicken stock	2¼ cups / 450 ml
Black peppercorns, crushed	10
Garlic cloves, crushed / roughly chopped	2/5
Pork, minced	125 gm
Black pepper	a pinch
Soy sauce	1½ tbsp / 25 ml
Bamboo shoots	100 gm
Fish sauce	3 tbsp / 45 ml

For the garnish

Spring onion, sliced	1
Green coriander	

Method:

1. In a saucepan, heat the chicken stock along with the black peppercorns and both the crushed and chopped garlic cloves.
2. Mix the pork with the black pepper and soy sauce. Make small balls and gently put them into the chicken stock. Cook for 4-5 minutes.
3. Serve garnished with spring onion and green coriander.

Tom Kha Kai

Chicken and ginger soup

Preparation time: 15 min.
Cooking time: 10 min.
Serves: 2-4

Ingredients:

Chicken, boneless cubes	360 gm
Coconut milk	3 cups / 600 ml
Mushrooms, sliced	120 gm
Kha	2 tbsp / 30 gm
Galangal	4 tbsp / 60 gm
Lemon grass, chopped	50 gm
Red chillies, chopped	4
Fish sauce	3 tbsp / 45 ml
Lemon juice	4 tbsp / 60 ml
Green coriander	4-6 sprigs
Chilli oil	1 tsp / 5 ml

Method:

1. Heat the coconut milk in a pan; add the mushrooms, kha, galangal, lemon grass and red chillies.
2. Stir in the fish sauce and lemon juice.
3. Boil for 5-6 minutes and remove from the heat.
4. Serve hot, garnished with green coriander and chilli oil.

Tom Kha Phak
Vegetable coconut soup

Preparation time: 10 min.
Cooking time: 15 min.
Serves: 2-4

Ingredients:

Coconut milk	2 cups / 400 ml
Carrots, sliced	120 gm
Cabbage, sliced	120 gm
Cauliflower, sliced	80 gm
Galangal	80 gm
Lemon grass, cut into diamonds	50 gm
Lemon leaves	6
Red chillies, cut into diamonds	4
Fish sauce and Salt to taste	
Lemon juice	4 tbsp / 60 ml
Chilli oil	2 tsp / 10 ml
Green coriander	4 sprigs

Method:

1. Heat a pan; add the coconut milk along with all the ingredients (except chilli oil) and green coriander.
2. Bring to a boil and cook for 5-10 minutes. Remove from the heat.
3. Serve hot, garnished with chilli oil and green coriander.

Tom Kha Kai (Veg)
Mildly spiced vegetable soup

Preparation time: 15 min.
Cooking time: 10 min.
Serves: 2-4

Ingredients:

Coconut milk	2 cups / 400 ml
Mushrooms, sliced	120 gm
Kha	2 tbsp / 30 gm
Galangal	5½ tbsp / 80 gm
Lemon grass, chopped	80 gm
Red chillies, chopped	4
Fish sauce	3 tbsp / 45 ml
Lemon juice	4 tbsp / 60 ml
Green coriander	4-6 sprigs
Chilli oil	1 tsp / 5 ml

Method:

1 Heat the coconut milk in a pan; add the mushrooms, kha, galangal, lemon grass and red chillies.
2. Stir in the fish sauce and lemon juice.
3. Boil for 5-6 minutes and then remove from the heat.
4. Serve hot, garnished with green coriander and chilli oil.

Tod Mun Kung
Prawn and corn fritters

Preparation time: 5 min.
Cooking time: 10 min.
Serves: 2-4

Ingredients:

Self-raising flour	4 tsp / 20 gm
Prawns, minced	65 gm
Red curry paste (see p. 7)	1 tsp / 5 gm
Corn kernels	¼ cup / 50 gm
Egg, white only	1
Lime leaf	1
Oil for deep-frying	
Green coriander sprigs to garnish	

Method:

1. In a bowl, mix the self-raising flour, prawns, red curry paste, corn kernels, egg white and lime leaf together.
2. Heat the oil in a wok; drop about 1 tbsp of the mixture at a time into the hot oil. Cook for about 5 minutes on moderate heat or until golden brown.
3. Remove the fritters from the wok and drain the excess oil on an absorbent paper.
4. Serve garnished with green coriander accompanied with a dipping sauce.

Peagai Yat Sai
Stuffed chicken wings

Preparation time: 35 min.
Cooking time: 25 min.
Serves: 2-4

Ingredients:

Chicken wings	8
Pork, minced	175 gm
Sugar	2 tsp / 10 gm
Soy sauce	2½ tbsp / 40 ml
Black pepper	a pinch
Onions, finely chopped	40 gm
Green peas	25 gm
Rice vermicelli, soaked for 15 minutes	50 gm
Oil for deep-frying	

Method:

1. Remove the main bones from the chicken wings by using a knife to loosen the meat around the top.
2. In a big bowl, add the pork, sugar, soy sauce, black pepper, onions, green peas and rice vermicelli. Mix thoroughly and keep the stuffing aside.
3. Fill each chicken wing with an equal amount of stuffing; seal properly so that the stuffing does not come out.
4. Place the stuffed wings in a steamer and steam for 15 minutes. Keep aside.
5. Heat the oil in a wok; deep-fry the steamed stuffed wings for about 6 minutes or until they are golden.
6. Serve hot.

Satay Kai
Marinated chicken on sticks

Preparation time: 4 hr. 20 min.
Cooking time: 10 min.
Serves: 2-4

Ingredients:

Chicken, boneless	600 gm
Curry powder	8 tsp / 40 gm
Garlic cloves	3 tbsp / 45 gm
Coriander root	8 tsp / 40 gm
Coriander seeds	1 tbsp / 15 gm
White pepper powder	4 tsp / 20 gm
Fish sauce	½ cup / 100 ml
Lemon grass, chopped	8 tsp / 40 gm
Kha, chopped	5 tsp / 25 gm
Cumin seeds	4 tsp / 20 gm
Peanut sauce	½ cup / 100 ml

Method:

1. Cut the chicken into 2" broad strips.
2. Make a paste by mixing together the curry powder, garlic cloves, coriander root, coriander seeds, white pepper powder, fish sauce, lemon grass, kha and cumin seeds.
3. Marinate the chicken strips in the prepared paste for 4 hours.
4. Skewer the chicken strips on bamboo sticks and grill / roast till the chicken is done.
5. Remove from the heat and serve hot, on the sticks themselves, accompanied by peanut sauce.

Yam Nuea

Spiced tenderloin delight

Preparation time: 20 min.
Cooking time: 5 min.
Serves: 2-4

Ingredients:

Veal tenderloin	600 gm
Garlic, chopped	40 gm
Red chillies, chopped	4
Green chillies, chopped	4
Lemon juice	3 tbsp / 45 ml
Fish sauce	3 tbsp / 45 ml
Onions, sliced	120 gm
Tomatoes, sliced	120 gm
Spring onions, sliced	80 gm
Mint leave sprigs	3-4

Method:

1. Grill the tenderloin until it is well done. Allow it to cool and then cut into strips.
2. Prepare a dressing by mixing together the garlic, red chillies and green chillies, lemon juice and fish sauce.
3. In a bowl, add the tenderloin along with the sliced vegetables.
4. Pour the prepared dressing on top and mix well.
5. Serve garnished with mint leaves.

Thord Man Koong

Seafood croquettes

Preparation time: 30 min.
Cooking time: 15 min.
Serves: 2-4

Ingredients:

Prawns, shelled, cleaned	400 gm
Pork fat	80 gm
Fish sauce	4 tbsp / 60 ml
Chinese wine	4 tsp / 20 ml
White pepper powder	2 tsp / 10 gm
Cornflour	4 tsp / 20 gm
Sesame oil	4 tsp / 20 ml
Light soy sauce	4 tsp / 20 ml
Breadcrumbs	1 cup / 200 gm
Oil for frying	

Method:

1. Mince the prawns and pork fat together.
2. To the prawn mixture, add the fish sauce, Chinese wine, white pepper powder, cornflour, sesame oil, soy sauce and mix well.
3. Shape the mixture into small round cutlets. Coat with breadcrumbs and deep-fry in hot oil until golden brown in colour.
4. Remove, drain the excess oil and place neatly on a serving platter.
5. Serve hot, accompanied by *Nam Jim Buey* sauce (see p. 86).

Prik Yat Sai
Stuffed peppers

Preparation time: 15 min.
Cooking time: 30 min.
Serves: 2-4

Ingredients:

Peppers, red / green / yellow, cored, deseeded	4
Garlic pods	5
Coriander roots	8
Pork, minced	275 gm
Soy sauce	1 tbsp / 15 ml
Black pepper, ground	½ tsp / 3 gm
Green coriander for garnish	

Method:

1. Pound the garlic and coriander roots in a mortar for about 2-3 minutes or till well broken.
2. In a big bowl, take the pork, add the pounded garlic and coriander roots along with soy sauce and black pepper. Mix well and keep aside for 7-8 minutes.
3. Fill the peppers with the pork stuffing and steam for about 30 minutes in a steamer.
4. Transfer the stuffed peppers into a dish; cut each into 3-4 slices and serve garnished with green coriander.

Thod Man Khow Phot

Sweetcorn cakes

Preparation time: 5 min.
Cooking time: 35 min.
Serves: 2-4

Ingredients:

Sweetcorn	350 gm
Green curry paste (see p. 7)	1 tbsp / 15 gm
Plain flour	2 tbsp / 30 gm
Rice flour	3 tbsp / 45 gm
Spring onions, finely chopped	3-4
Egg, beaten	1
Fish sauce	2 tsp / 10 ml
Oil for deep-frying	

Method:

1. In a blender or food processor, put the sweetcorn, green curry paste, plain flour, rice flour, spring onions, egg and fish sauce and blend until the sweetcorn is lightly chopped. Shape the mixture into equal-sized cakes.

2. Heat the oil in a wok; deep-fry the cakes a few at a time for 3 minutes or till golden brown.

3. Drain the excess oil and serve with *Sieuw* sauce (see p. 86).

Som Tum
Raw papaya salad

Preparation time: 15 min.
Serves: 2-4

Ingredients:

Raw papaya, shredded	1 kg
Tomatoes, chopped	240 gm
Peanuts	180 gm
Garlic cloves	6-8
Red chillies, whole	6
Fish sauce to taste	
Lemon juice	3 tbsp / 45 ml
Sugar	2 tbsp / 30 gm

Method:

1. Pound the peanuts, garlic cloves and red chillies in a mortar and pestle. Transfer into a bowl.
2. Add the papaya to the peanut mixture along with the tomatoes, fish sauce, lemon juice and sugar. Mix well.
3. Remove into a serving dish and serve immediately.

Por Pia Savoey
Thai spring rolls

Preparation time: 25 min.
Cooking time: 10 min.
Serves: 2-4

Ingredients:

Vermicelli, soaked for 10 minutes	120 gm
Cabbage, shredded	120 gm
Carrots, shredded	60 gm
Spring onions, shredded	40 gm
Onions, shredded	60 gm
Oil	4 tbsp / 60 ml
Salt to taste	
Pepper to taste	
Soy sauce	2 tsp / 10 ml
Spring roll skins	16
Plum sauce	½ cup / 100 ml

Method:

1. Heat 1 tbsp oil in a pan; add the vegetables and sauté for a few minutes.
2. Add the vermicelli, salt and pepper to taste and the soy sauce. Sauté further for a few seconds.
3. Remove from the heat and place on a perforated vessel to allow it to cool. Divide the mixture into 4 equal portions.
4. Roll the portions into the spring roll skins and deep-fry in hot oil. Remove and keep aside.
5. Serve hot, accompanied by *Nam Jim Buey* sauce (see p. 86).

Pla Thod Krathieum Prik Thai

Deep-fried crispy pomfret

Preparation time: 35 min.
Cooking time: 20 min.
Serves: 2-4

Ingredients:

Pomfret, whole	350 gm / 1
Fish sauce	2 tbsp / 30 ml
Garlic	2 tsp / 10 gm
Cornflour	4 tbsp / 60 gm
Oil for frying	
Red chillies, chopped	3
Kaffir leaves, chopped	3
Red curry paste (see p. 7)	4 tbsp / 60 gm
Oyster sauce	3 tsp / 15 ml
Sugar	1 tsp / 5 gm
Lemon juice	2 tbsp / 30 ml
Green coriander	6-8 sprigs

Method:

1. Clean the pomfret, remove its fins and cut the belly. Make gashes across it.
2. Marinate it in fish sauce and garlic for 20 minutes.
3. Dissolve the cornflour in water and keep aside.
4. Heat the oil; coat the pomfret with the cornflour solution and fry until crisp and golden brown. Drain the excess oil and keep aside.
5. Reheat 2 tbsp oil in a wok; add the red curry paste along with red chillies, kaffir leaves, oyster sauce, sugar and lemon juice.
6. Sauté on high heat for a few minutes.
7. Place the pomfret on a serving platter and pour the prepared sauce on top. Garnish with sprigs of green coriander and serve hot.

Seafood

36

Hor Mok Thalay

Seafood baked in a coconut shell

Preparation time: 20 min.
Cooking time: 30 min.
Serves: 2-4

Ingredients:

Tender coconuts	2
Fish	150 gm
Prawns	150 gm
Squid	100 gm
Red curry paste (see p. 7)	¾ cup / 150 gm
Kaffir leaves	6-8
Basil leaves	6-8
Lemon grass	8 tsp / 40 gm
Galangal	8 tsp / 40 gm
Coconut milk	1 cup / 200 ml
Red chilies	3
Eggs, whisked	2
Green coriander to garnish	

(Photograph on front cover)

Method:

1. Cut open the top of the tender coconut, remove the coconut milk and keep aside.
2. Mix the fish along with the prawns, squid, red curry paste, kaffir leaves, basil leaves, lemon grass, galangal, coconut milk and red chillies.
3. Fill the tender coconut with the prepared mixture and pour the whisked egg on top.
4. Place the coconut on a tray and steam for about 25 minutes.
5. Remove the coconut from the steamer, garnish with green coriander and serve hot, accompanied by steamed rice.

Gang Som Pla

Hot and sour fish curry

Preparation time: 5 min.
Cooking time: 30 min.
Serves: 2-4

Ingredients:

White fish, (haddock / cod), firm,
   boneless   150 gm
Red curry paste (see p. 7)   1 tbsp / 15 gm
Fish stock   4½ cups / 900 ml
Baby corn cobs, obliquely sliced   4
Chinese leaves, chopped   100 gm
Sugar   2 tbsp / 30 gm
Fish sauce   5 tbsp / 75 ml
Tamarind, softened in 150 ml
   hot water   40 gm

Method:

1. Poach the fish in a pan of gently simmering water for 10-15 minutes or till cooked.

2. Remove the fish out of the pan and discard the skin. Put the flesh in the mortar and pound until it is soft and pulpy. Add the red curry paste and mix well.

3. In a saucepan, heat the fish stock. Add the fish paste and bring to a boil, stirring constantly.

4. Reduce the heat and add the baby corn cobs, Chinese leaves, sugar and fish sauce. Simmer gently for 10 minutes.

5. Stir in the tamarind water, simmer for another 5 minutes and serve.

Gung Pad Kratien

Stir-fried prawns with garlic

Preparation time: 15 min.
Cooking time: 5 min.
Serves: 4

Seafood

Ingredients:

Prawns, shelled	12
Oil	1 tbsp / 15 ml
Onions, finely sliced	50 gm
Garlic, minced	1 tbsp / 15 gm
Black pepper, ground	1 tbsp / 15 gm
Broccoli stems, peeled, sliced	50 gm
Mushrooms, sliced	25 gm
Fish stock	4-6 tbsp / 60-90 ml
Soy sauce	4 tbsp / 60 ml
Green coriander, chopped	1 tbsp / 15 gm

Method:

1. Heat the oil in a wok; add the onions, garlic and black pepper and stir-fry for 30 seconds.
2. Add the broccoli stems and stir-fry for 1 minute. Add the mushrooms, prawns, 4 tbsp fish stock and soy sauce. Stir-fry over high heat for 1-2 minutes adding more fish stock if the mixture is drying out.
3. Serve hot, garnished with green coriander.

Phad Hoy Lai

Seafood with chilli and basil

Preparation time: 15 min.
Cooking time: 35 min.
Serves: 2-4

Ingredients:

Mussels, in shells	16
Squids, cleaned, cubed	250 gm
Oil	1 tbsp / 15 ml
Garlic cloves, chopped	2
Spring onions, sliced	6
Basil leaves, fresh	20
Fish sauce	2 tbsp / 30 ml
Soy sauce	1 tbsp / 15 ml
Red / green chilli, deseeded chopped	1
Brown sugar	1 tbsp / 15 gm
Prawns, peeled, uncooked	200 gm

Method:

1. Scrub the mussels, remove any dirt or beard and rinse well.
2. Heat the oil in a large saucepan; add the garlic and spring onions and fry for 1 minute.
3. Add the remaining ingredients except the squids and prawns. Cook covered for 6 minutes. Mussels which do not open should be discarded.
4. Add the squids and prawns and cook for 3-4 minutes or till they are cooked. Serve hot.

Kaeng Phet Koong

Prawns in red curry

Preparation time: 20 min.
Cooking time: 10 min.
Serves: 2-4

Ingredients:

Prawns, cleaned, deveined	400 gm
Bamboo shoots, chopped	60 gm
White pumpkin, quartered	40 gm
Red chillies, quartered	4
Mushrooms, sliced	60 gm
Oil	4 tbsp / 60 ml
Red curry paste (see p. 7)	¾ cup / 150 gm
Kaffir leaves	6-8 sprigs
Basil leaves	6-8
Coconut milk	1 cup / 200 ml
Fish sauce	3 tbsp / 45 ml
Sugar	4 tsp / 20 gm

Method:

1. Blanch the bamboo shoots and keep aside.
2. Heat the oil in a pan; add the red curry paste and cook for 2-3 minutes.
3. Add the kaffir leaves along with all the vegetables, basil leaves, coconut milk, fish sauce and sugar.
4. Cook on low heat for 5-10 minutes.
5. Remove from the heat and serve hot, accompanied by steamed rice.

Kai Yang
Grilled whole chicken

Preparation time: 15 min.
Cooking time: 20 min.
Serves: 2-4

Ingredients:

Chicken	1½ kg
Lemon grass, chopped	8 tsp / 40 gm
Galangal, chopped	8 tsp / 40 gm
Coriander root	¼ cup / 50 gm
Garlic, chopped	8 tsp / 40 gm
Fish sauce	3 tbsp / 45 ml
White pepper powder	1 tbsp / 15 gm
Soy sauce	4 tsp / 20 ml
Kao wine	4 tsp / 20 ml
Sweet chilli sauce	4 tbsp / 60 ml

Method:

1. Mix all the vegetables along with fish sauce, white pepper powder, soy sauce, Kao wine and sweet chilli sauce. Blend to make a smooth paste.
2. Cut the backbone of the chicken into two and flatten.
3. Marinate the chicken in the prepared paste and keep aside for 4-5 hours.
4. Skewer the chicken and grill over a charcoal grill until it is cooked.
5. Remove from the skewers and serve hot, accompanied by steamed rice and *Tom Yam Koong* (see p. 10).

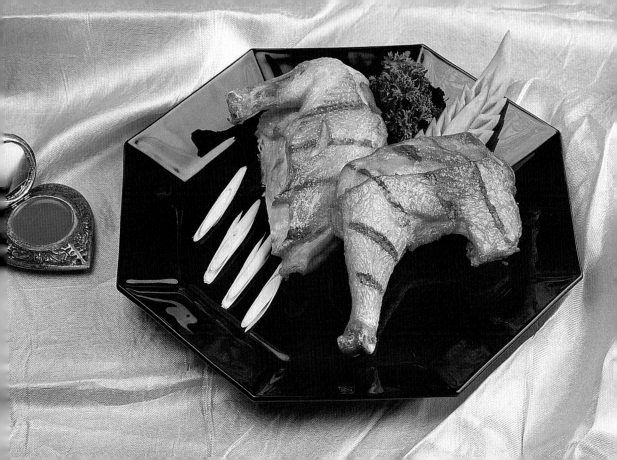

Kai Yad Sai
Chicken omelette

Preparation time: 25 min.
Cooking time: 10 min.
Serves: 2-4

Ingredients:

Chicken, minced	200 gm
Oil	¾ cup / 150 ml
Mushrooms, chopped	360 gm
Carrots, chopped	180 gm
Onions, chopped	180 gm
Capsicums, chopped	80 gm
Baby corn, chopped	80 gm
Green peas	180 gm
Tomato ketchup	3 tbsp / 45 ml
Fish sauce	2 tbsp / 30 ml
Oyster sauce	1 tsp / 5 ml
Maggi sauce (optional)	1 tsp / 5 ml
Soy sauce	2 tsp / 10 ml
Pepper powder	1 tsp / 5 gm
Eggs, whisked	3

Method:

1. Reserve 4 tsp oil and heat the rest in a wok. Sauté the chicken mince until light brown.
2. Add the vegetables along with mushrooms, tomato ketchup, fish sauce, oyster sauce, Maggi sauce, soy sauce and pepper powder.
3. Mix well and cook until the vegetables are tender. Remove from the heat and keep aside.
4. Heat the reserved oil in a pan; add the beaten eggs to make a thin omelette. Remove and keep aside.
5. Place the prepared mixture in the centre of the omelette and fold like a parcel.
6. Remove to a dish and serve.

Kai Phad Khing

Stir-fried chicken

Preparation time: 20 min.
Cooking time: 10 min.
Serves: 2-4

Chicken

Ingredients:

Chicken	800 gm
Oil	¾ cup / 150 ml
Garlic, chopped	20 gm
Pineapple, quartered	240 gm
Capsicums, quartered	120 gm
Onions, quartered	60 gm
Spring onions, quartered	40 gm
Red chillies, quartered	6-8
Mushrooms, sliced	60 gm
Ginger, shredded	60 gm
Oyster sauce	4 tsp / 20 ml
Fish sauce	4 tsp / 20 ml
Chicken stock	3 tbsp / 45 ml

(Photograph on page 2)

Method:

1. Cut the chicken into strips and blanch it.
2. Heat the oil in a wok; sauté the garlic, add the chicken along with the remaining ingredients.
3. Toss on high heat for a few minutes; reduce the heat and cook till the vegetables are tender.
4. Remove from the heat and serve hot, accompanied by steamed rice.

Gang Keyo Wun Gai

Chicken in green curry

Preparation time: 7 min.
Cooking time: 15 min.
Serves: 2-4

Ingredients:

Chicken breasts, cubed	125 gm
Oil	1 tbsp / 15 ml
Green curry paste (see p. 7)	1½ tbsp / 25 gm
Coconut milk	4 tbsp / 60 ml
Lime leaves, torn	2
Lemon grass, cut in oblique slices	½ stalk
Bamboo shoots	50 gm
Aubergines, small, round, quartered	3
Courgette, cut in oblique chunks	50 gm
Red chilli, large, obliquely sliced	1
Chicken stock	6 tbsp / 90 ml
Brown sugar	1 tbsp / 15 gm
Fish sauce	3 tbsp / 45 ml
Basil sprigs to garnish	

Method:

1. Heat the oil in a wok; add the green curry paste and cook for 30 seconds. Add the coconut milk and cook for 1 minute, stirring continuously.
2. Add the chicken and let it simmer for a while. Add all the remaining ingredients and let it simmer for 10 minutes more, stirring occasionally.
3. Serve hot, garnished with basil sprigs.

Panaeng Kai
Chicken in red curry

Preparation time: 15 min.
Cooking time: 15 min.
Serves: 2-4

Chicken

Ingredients:

Chicken	800 gm
Panaeng curry paste	5 tbsp / 80 gm
Coconut milk	1 cup / 200 ml
Basil leaves	8-10
Kaffir leaves	5
Fish sauce	4 tbsp / 60 ml
Red chillies	3
Green chillies	3

Method:

1. Cut the chicken into strips.
2. Heat a pan; add the Panaeng curry paste, chicken strips and coconut milk. Cook for 4-5 minutes.
3. Add the basil leaves, kaffir leaves, fish sauce, red and green chillies. Mix well and simmer for 10 minutes (if required, stir in the chicken stock).
4. Remove from the heat and serve hot.

Kaeng Karee Kai

Chicken in yellow curry

Preparation time: 15 min.
Cooking time: 15 min.
Serves: 2-4

Ingredients:

Chicken	800 gm
Oil	¾ cup / 150 ml
Yellow curry paste (see p. 9)	6 tbsp / 80 gm
Onions	120 gm
Coconut milk	1 cup / 200 ml
Fish sauce	4 tbsp / 60 ml
Sugar	2 tbsp / 30 gm
Salt to taste	

Method:

1. Cut the chicken into strips.
2. Heat the oil in a pan; add the yellow curry paste and onions, sauté for 2-3 minutes.
3. Stir in the remaining ingredients and cook on low heat for 15 minutes (if required add a little chicken stock).
4. Stir in the salt to taste and remove from the heat.
5. Serve hot, accompanied by steamed rice.

Chicken

Patani
Stir-fried lamb

Preparation time: 20 min.
Cooking time: 10 min.
Serves: 2-4

Ingredients:

Lamb	800 gm
Oil	¾ cup / 150 ml
Garlic, chopped	40 gm
Capsicums, chopped	80 gm
Onions, chopped	60 gm
Red chillies, chopped	4-6
Spring onions, chopped	60 gm
Ginger, shredded	80 gm
Fish sauce	2 tsp / 10 ml
Oyster sauce	2 tsp / 10 ml
Light soy sauce	1 tsp / 5 ml
Pepper powder	1 tsp / 5 gm

Method:

1. Cut the lamb into slices, blanch and keep aside.
2. Heat the oil in a wok; add the garlic and sauté until light brown.
3. Add the capsicums, onions, red chillies and spring onions along with ginger and sauté for a minute.
4. Stir in the fish sauce, oyster sauce, light soy sauce and pepper powder. Toss on high heat for 5 minutes.
5. Transfer into a serving dish and serve hot.

Lamb

Kaeng Khreo Wan Nuea

Lamb in green curry

Preparation time: 10 min.
Cooking time: 15 min.
Serves: 2-4

Ingredients:

Lamb	800 gm
Oil	¾ cup / 120 ml
Green curry paste (see p. 7)	½ cup / 100 gm
Pia aubergines	120 gm
Kaffir leaves	4-6
Red chillies	4
Basil leaves	6-8
Coconut milk	1 cup / 200 ml
Fish sauce	3 tbsp / 45 ml
Sugar	4 tsp / 20 gm
Salt to taste	

Method:

1. Cut the lamb into slices.
2. Heat the oil in a pan; add the green curry paste along with the sliced lamb and sauté for 2-3 minutes.
3. Stir in the pia aubergines, kaffir leaves, red chillies, basil leaves, coconut milk, fish sauce and sugar.
4. Cook on low heat for 15 minutes (if required add a little chicken stock).
5. Add the salt to taste and serve hot, accompanied by steamed rice.

Lamb

Kaeng Phae

Lamb with mint

Preparation time: 20 min.
Cooking time: 15 min.
Serves: 2-4

Ingredients:

Lamb, thinly sliced	500 gm
Aubergine, medium, cubed	1
Garlic cloves, chopped	2
Salt	2 tbsp / 30 gm
Oil	2 tbsp / 30 ml
Red chilli, deseeded, chopped	1
Fish sauce	2 tbsp / 30 ml
Brown sugar	1 tbsp / 15 gm
Water	5½ tbsp / 80 ml
Mint leaves, fresh	20

Method:

1. Place the aubergine in a colander and sprinkle with salt. Mix well and leave it to drain for 20 minutes. Rinse under cold water and drain well.

2. Heat the oil in a large frying pan; add the lamb and garlic and fry till well browned.

3. Add the aubergine and red chilli, stir-fry over moderate heat for 5 minutes.

4. Mix in the fish sauce, brown sugar, water and mint leaves and fry for 1 minute or till the aubergine is soft. If the sauce becomes too thick add some more water.

5. Serve hot accompanied with steamed rice.

Phad Phak Bai Krapaw

Mixed vegetables

Preparation time: 20 min.
Cooking time: 10 min.
Serves: 2-4

Ingredients:

Mushrooms, sliced	120 gm
Carrots, sliced	240 gm
Cabbage, diced	240 gm
Baby corn	240 gm
Broccoli, cut into florets	240 gm
Cauliflower, cut into florets	240 gm
Oil	¾ cup / 150 ml
Garlic, chopped	20 gm
Green chillies, chopped	3
Red chillies, chopped	3
Salt to taste	
Basil leaves	10-12
Soy sauce	2 tsp / 10 ml
Oyster sauce	2 tsp / 10 ml

Method:

1. Blanch all the vegetables along with the baby corn. Keep aside.
2. Heat the oil in a wok; add the garlic, green and red chillies and sauté for a few minutes.
3. Add all the vegetables along with the salt, basil leaves (keep aside a few for garnishing), soy sauce and oyster sauce. Toss well for a few minutes and then remove from the heat.
4. Serve hot, garnished with basil leaves.

Panaeng Tao Hoo Kap Het

Stir-fried tofu with mushrooms

Preparation time: 15 min.
Cooking time: 15 min.
Serves: 2-4

Ingredients:

Tofu, diced	500 gm
Oil for frying	
Mushrooms, cut into halves	300 gm
Panaeng curry paste	1 cup / 200 gm
Capsicums, diced	120 gm
Onions, diced	120 gm
Coconut milk	2 cups / 400 ml
Lemon leaves	6
Basil leaves	10-12
Fish sauce to taste	
Salt to taste	
Red chillies	4
Green chillies	4

Method:

1. Heat the oil in a pan and deep-fry the tofu till golden brown. Drain the excess oil and keep aside.
2. Blanch the mushrooms and keep aside.
3. In a pan, heat the Panaeng curry paste; add the fried tofu, mushrooms, capsicums and onions. Sauté for a minute.
4. Stir in the coconut milk and bring to a boil. Add the remaining ingredients and cook on low heat for 10 minutes (if required add the vegetable stock).
5. Serve hot, accompanied by steamed rice.

Phad Phak Kaeng Dang

Red curry vegetables

Preparation time: 15 min.
Cooking time: 30 min.
Serves: 8

Vegetarian

Ingredients:

Red curry paste (see p. 7) 2-3 tbsp / 30-45 gm
Potatoes, chopped   4
Pumpkin / carrots, chopped   300 gm
Sweet potatoes, chopped   400 gm
Vegetable stock   2½ cups / 500 ml
Cauliflower, broken into florets   300 gm
Green beans, trimmed   250 gm

Method:

1. In a large saucepan, cook the red curry paste over medium heat for 2 minutes.
2. Add the potatoes, pumpkin / carrots, sweet potatoes and vegetable stock and bring to a boil. Simmer, stirring occasionally, for 20 minutes or till the vegetables are cooked.
3. Add the cauliflower and green beans and cook for 3-5 minutes longer or till the vegetables are tender. Serve hot.

Phad Fak Thong

Pumpkin with chilli and garlic

Preparation time: 10 min.
Cooking time: 35 min.
Serves: 6-8

Ingredients:

Pumpkin, peeled, thinly sliced	500 gm
Oil	3 tbsp / 45 ml
Onion, chopped	1
Garlic cloves, crushed	2
Eggs	3
Green chilli, deseeded, chopped	1
Fish sauce	2 tsp / 10 ml

Method:

1. Heat the oil in a large frying pan; add the pumpkin, onion and garlic and fry over moderate heat till the pumpkin is soft, stirring occasionally.
2. Beat the eggs, green chilli and fish sauce together and pour over the pumpkin. Cook covered till the egg is set.
3. Cut into wedges and serve hot.

Phad Phak Ruam Mit

Stir-fried vegetables

Preparation time: 20 min.
Cooking time: 10 min.
Serves: 2-4

Vegetarian

Ingredients:

Carrots, diced	200 gm
Cabbage, chopped	240 gm
Cauliflower, small florets	240 gm
Baby corn	240 gm
Mushrooms, cut into halves	240 gm
Cooking oil	½ cup / 100 ml
Garlic	40 gm
Soy sauce	2 tsp / 10 ml
Salt to taste	
Pepper powder to taste	
Sugar	a pinch

Method:

1. Blanch all the vegetables including the baby corn. Keep aside.
2. Heat the oil in a wok; add the garlic and sauté.
3. Add the blanched vegetables and sauté further over high heat.
4. Stir in the soy sauce, salt to taste, pepper to taste and sugar. Mix well.
5. Remove from the heat and serve hot.

Phad Het Kap Met Mamaung

Stir-fried mushrooms

Preparation time: 40 min.
Cooking time: 15 min.
Serves: 2-4

Ingredients:

Mushrooms, cut into quarters	600 gm
Cashewnuts	240 gm
Oil	¾ cup / 150 ml
Garlic, chopped	4 tsp / 20 gm
Onions, cut into discs	120 gm
Capsicums, cut into discs	80 gm
Red chillies, dry, roasted	4
Spring onions, chopped	120 gm
Green chillies, chopped	2
Salt to taste	
Pepper to taste	

Method:

1. Blanch the mushrooms and keep aside. Fry the cashewnuts till golden brown.
2. Heat the oil in a wok; sauté the garlic. Add the remaining ingredients and toss on high heat for a few minutes. Add a little stock if required.
3. Serve hot, accompanied by steamed rice.

Khao Phad Phak
Vegetable fried rice

Preparation time: 30 min.
Cooking time: 20 min.
Serves: 2-4

Ingredients:

Steamed rice	600 gm
Cabbage, diced	80 gm
Carrots, chopped	80 gm
Green peas	80 gm
Mushrooms, halved	80 gm
Broccoli, cut into florets	80 gm
Cauliflower, cut into florets	80 gm
Oil	¾ cup / 150 ml
Garlic, chopped	10 gm
Salt to taste	
Pepper to taste	
Soy sauce	2 tsp / 10 ml

Method:

1. Blanch the cabbage, carrots, green peas, mushrooms along with broccoli and cauliflower. Remove from the heat and keep aside.
2. Heat the oil in a wok and sauté the garlic. Stir in the remaining ingredients and toss on high heat for a few minutes.
3. Remove from the heat and serve hot.

Khao Phad Bai Krapaw Kai

Chicken fried rice

Preparation time: 30 min.
Cooking time: 15 min.
Serves: 2-4

Ingredients:

Steamed rice	600 gm
Chicken strips	240 gm
Oil	¾ cup / 150 ml
Red chillies, chopped	4
Green chillies, chopped	4
Garlic, chopped	20 gm
Basil leaves	20
Soy sauce	2 tsp / 10 ml
Spring onions, cut into strips	240 gm

Method:

1. Blanch the chicken strips and keep aside.
2. Heat the oil in a wok; sauté the red chillies, green chillies and garlic.
3. Add the chicken strips and sauté. Stir in the remaining ingredients and toss well for a few seconds.
4. Serve hot, garnished with spring onions.

Khao Phad Sapparod
Pineapple-chicken fried rice

Preparation time: 10 min.
Cooking time: 10 min.
Serves: 2-4

Ingredients:

Steamed rice	600 gm
Chicken	120 gm
Pineapple, chopped	120 gm
Oil	¾ cup / 150 ml
Garlic	20 gm
Green peas	120 gm
Spring onions, chopped	60 gm
Raisins	2 tbsp / 30 gm
Soy sauce	2 tsp / 10 ml
Salt to taste	
Pepper to taste	
Sugar	a pinch
Cashewnuts, crushed	40 gm

Method:

1. Blanch the chicken and keep aside.
2. Heat the oil in a wok; add the garlic and sauté for a few minutes. Mix in the green peas, spring onions, pineapple, chicken and raisins. Toss for a while.
3. Stir in the steamed rice, soy sauce, salt, pepper and sugar. Mix well.
4. Remove from the heat and serve hot, garnished with cashewnuts.

Khao Kaeng Dang

Red curry rice

Preparation time: 5 min.
Cooking time: 30 min.
Serves: 4

Ingredients:

Rice, long-grain	1 cup / 200 gm
Oil	2 tbsp / 30 ml
Red curry paste (see p. 7)	1 tbsp / 15 gm
Green coriander, chopped	4-5 tbsp
Water	2½ cups / 500 ml
Soy sauce	1½ tbsp / 25 ml

Method:

1. Heat the oil in a large saucepan. Add the rice and fry until golden brown for about 4 minutes. Stir occasionally.
2. Add the red curry paste and fry for 1 minute.
3. Add the green coriander, water and soy sauce and bring to a boil. Now turn the heat to very low and cook covered for 10 minutes.
4. Remove from the heat and allow the rice to stand for 5 minutes before serving.

Khao Phad Krueng

Spiced rice

Preparation time: 5 min.
Cooking time: 30 min.
Serves: 4

Ingredients:

Rice, long-grain	1 cup / 200 gm
Butter	1 tbsp / 15 gm
Onion, chopped	1
Red / green chilli, deseeded, chopped	1
Cumin seeds	1 tsp / 5 gm
Fish sauce	1 tbsp / 15 ml
Water	2½ cups / 500 ml

Method:

1. In a large saucepan, melt the butter. Add the onion, red / green chilli and cumin seeds. Fry for 3-4 minutes on moderate heat.

2. Add the fish sauce, rice and water and bring to a boil. Cook covered on low heat for 10 minutes. Remove from the heat and allow the mixture to stand for 5 minutes.

3. Serve hot.

Guey Tiew Phat Khee Mao

Stir-fried noodles

Preparation time: 40 min.
Cooking time: 15 min.
Serves: 2-4

Ingredients:

Rice noodles	500 gm
Oil	¾ cup / 150 ml
Garlic, chopped	40 gm
Green chillies, chopped	6
Lemon grass, chopped	30 gm
Galangal, chopped	30 gm
Chicken, julienned	120 gm
Spring onions, cut into strips	180 gm
Basil leaves, chopped	20-30
Fish sauce	2 tbsp / 30 ml
Oyster sauce	4 tsp / 20 ml
Soy sauce	1 tsp / 5 ml

Method:

1. Soak the rice noodles in water for 25 minutes. Drain and keep aside.
2. Blanch the chicken and keep aside.
3. In a wok, heat the oil and add the garlic, green chillies, lemon grass and galangal.
4. Sauté for a few minutes and then add the chicken. Sauté further for a few seconds and stir in the remaining ingredients.
5. Mix well and toss on high heat for a few seconds. Remove and serve hot.

Phad Thai
Traditional Thai noodles

Preparation time: 30 min.
Cooking time: 20 min.
Serves: 2-4

Ingredients:

Phad Thai noodles	400 gm
Tofu	120 gm
Oil	¾ cup / 150 ml
Preserved vegetables, chopped	45 gm
Prawns, cleaned, blanched	10
Garlic cloves	25 gm
Red chillies, pounded	2 tsp / 10 gm
Lemon juice	4 tbsp / 60 ml
Tamarind extract	2 tbsp / 30 ml
Sugar	4 tsp / 20 gm
Fish sauce	2 tbsp / 30 ml
Tomato ketchup	4 tbsp / 60 ml
Peanuts, crushed	50 gm
Lemon wedges to garnish	
Beansprouts	¼ cup / 50 gm

Method:

1. Soak the noodles in water for half an hour; drain and keep aside.
2. Cut the tofu into 1″ batons and deep-fry in hot oil.
3. Heat 2 tbsp oil in a wok; add the noodles along with the remaining ingredients (except peanuts) and toss well on high heat.
4. Remove from the heat and add the peanuts; return to the heat and toss well.
5. Serve hot, garnished with lemon wedges and beansprouts.

Yam Woon Sen
Vermicelli and shrimp salad

Preparation time: 20 min.
Cooking time: 10 min.
Serves: 2-4

Ingredients:

Rice vermicelli	400 gm
Water as required	
Onions, sliced	120 gm
Spring onions, sliced	120 gm
Red chillies, sliced	4
Green chillies, sliced	4
Mushrooms, sliced	120 gm
Prawns, cleaned, halved	240 gm
Carrots, julienned	80 gm
Ginger, julienned	80 gm
Celery, julienned	60 gm
Oil	4 tbsp / 60 ml
Water	4 tbsp / 60 ml
Fish sauce to taste	
Lemon juice	3 tbsp / 45 ml
Sugar	4 tbsp / 60 gm

Method:

1. Soak the rice vermicelli in water for 15 minutes. Drain and keep aside.
2. Heat the oil in a pan; add all the vegetables and prawns along with 4 tbsp water.
3. Stir in the fish sauce, lemon juice and sugar. Cook for 2 minutes or until the vegetables are tender.
4. Remove from the heat and serve.

Baa Mee Phad Thalay
Stir-fried noodles with seafood

Preparation time: 20 min.
Cooking time: 15 min.
Serves: 2-4

Ingredients:

Egg noodles	500 gm
Squids, cleaned, diced	100 gm
Prawns, cleaned, diced	100 gm
Sea fish, cleaned, diced	100 gm
Oil	¾ cup / 120 ml
Garlic cloves, chopped	3
Mushrooms, chopped	120 gm
Pepper powder	a pinch
Nam pla	2 tsp / 10 ml
Soy sauce	1 tsp / 5 ml
Oyster sauce	1 tsp / 5 ml
Spring onions, chopped	60 gm

Method:

1. Boil the noodles in sufficient water (add a little oil to prevent them from sticking). Drain and cool.
2. Blanch the squids, prawns and sea fish and keep aside.
3. Heat the oil in a wok; add the garlic and sauté for a few seconds.
4. Add the squids, prawns and sea fish along with mushrooms and noodles. Toss well.
5. Mix in the pepper powder, *Nam pla*, soy sauce, oyster sauce and toss on high heat for a few minutes.
6. Remove from the heat and add spring onions. Serve hot.

Baa Mee Phad Phak

Stir-fried vegetable noodles

Preparation time: 30 min.
Cooking time: 10 min.
Serves: 2-4

Ingredients:

Egg noodles	500 gm
Carrots, sliced	120 gm
Cauliflower, cut into florets	120 gm
Mushrooms, sliced	120 gm
Baby corn	120 gm
Oil	¾ cups / 150 ml
Garlic, chopped	12 gm
Salt to taste	
Pepper to taste	
Soy sauce	2 tsp / 10 ml
Oyster sauce	2 tsp / 10 ml
Spring onions, chopped	60 gm

Method:

1. Boil the noodles in sufficient water. Drain and cool. Add a little oil to the noodles to prevent them from sticking.
2. Blanch all the vegetables except spring onions and keep aside.
3. Heat the oil in a wok; sauté the garlic and add all the vegetables and noodles. Toss well.
4. Mix in salt, pepper, soy sauce, oyster sauce and toss over high heat.
5. Remove from the heat and stir in the spring onions. Serve hot.

Mee Krob
Crispy noodles

Preparation time: 6 min.
Cooking time: 35 min.
Serves: 4

Ingredients:

Tamarind pod, soaked, squeezed
   in 300 ml hot water   40 gm
Sugar   1 cup / 200 gm
Tomato ketchup   3 tbsp / 45 ml
Fish sauce   3 tbsp / 45 ml
Oil for deep-frying
Rice vermicelli   125 gm
Tofu, cubed   40 gm
Spring onion tops, sliced to garnish

Method:

1. Heat the tamarind water in a wok; add the sugar, stir till it dissolves. Add the tomato ketchup and fish sauce. Cook for 20-25 minutes, stirring till the sauce gradually thickens and is almost the consistency of jam. Remove from the heat and allow the sauce to cool a little.

2. In a another wok, heat the oil. When it is hot enough, deep-fry the noodles. They will puff up and expand immediately. Remove them with a slotted spoon and drain the excess oil.

3. Fry the tofu pieces and keep aside.

4. Put all the fried noodles in a large bowl. Pour the sweet red sauce over them. Add the tofu pieces and garnish with spring onion tops.

Sieuw Sauce

Soy and vinegar dipping sauce

Preparation time: 2 min.

Ingredients:

White vinegar	3 tbsp / 45 ml
Soy sauce	3 tbsp / 45 ml
Castor sugar	2 tsp / 10 gm
Red chillies, fresh, finely sliced	2

Method:

1. Combine all the ingredients in a bowl.
2. Stir continuously till the sugar dissolves.

Nam Jim Buey Sauce

Plum sauce

Preparation time: 1 min. Cooking time: 2 min.

Ingredients:

White vinegar	5 tbsp / 75 ml
Plum jam	4 tbsp / 60 gm
Red chilli, fresh, finely sliced	1

Method:

1. In a small pan, add the white vinegar and plum jam. Heat gently for 2 minutes, mixing continuously. Remove from the heat and allow it to cool.
2. Before serving add the red chilli.

Nam Gym Satay

Satay sauce

Prep. time: 1 min.   Cooking time: 15 min.

Ingredients:

Oil	1 tbsp / 15 ml
Red curry paste (see p. 7)	2 tsp / 10 gm
Coconut milk	3 tbsp / 45 ml
Water	125 ml
Brown sugar	3 tbsp / 45 gm
Peanuts, crushed	125 gm

Method:

1. Heat the oil in wok; add the red curry paste. Cook for 30 seconds and then add the remaining ingredients.
2. If the sauce becomes too thick add some more water.

Phet Waan Sauce

Hot and sweet sauce

Preparation time: 1 min. Cooking time: 2 min.

Ingredients:

White vinegar	½ cup / 100 ml
Brown sugar	4 tbsp / 60 gm
Salt	a pinch
Green chilli, fresh, finely chopped	1
Red chilli, fresh, finely chopped	1

Method:

1. Gently heat the white vinegar over low heat in a saucepan. Add the brown sugar and salt. Cook till the sugar has dissolved. Remove from the heat and allow it to cool.
2. Before serving, add the green and red chillies.

Kratiem Dong
Pickled garlic

Preparation time: 30 min.
Cooking time: 10 min.
Serves: 4

Ingredients:

Garlic bulbs, peeled	6
Water	6 cups / 1.2 lt
White vinegar	1½ cups / 300 ml
Sugar, granulated	¼ cup / 50 gm
Salt	1 tbsp / 15 gm

Method:

1. In a saucepan, bring the water, white vinegar, sugar and salt to a boil. Then reduce the heat and simmer for 5 minutes.
2. Add the garlic cloves, increase the flame and boil continuously for 1 minute.
3. Remove the saucepan from the heat and allow the garlic mixture to cool.
4. When cooled transfer into airtight containers and refrigerate for 10 days before eating.

Dong Tangkwa

Fresh cucumber pickle

Preparation time: 2 min.
Cooking time: 4 min.
Serves: 4

Ingredients:

Cucumber, large, peeled, halved lengthwise and sliced	1
Shallots, thinly sliced	1
Water	5 tbsp / 75 ml
Sugar, granulated	2 tbsp / 30 gm
White vinegar	2½ tbsp / 40 ml
Red chilli powder	a pinch
Salt	a pinch

Method:

1. In a saucepan heat the water. Add the sugar and stir until dissolved. Remove the saucepan from the heat and let the sugar syrup cool a little before adding the vinegar, red chilli and salt.
2. Pour the mixture in a bowl; add the cucumber and shallots and mix well.
3. Refrigerate for 4-5 days in an airtight container.

Khing Dong
Pickled ginger

Preparation time: **40 min.**
Cooking time: **20 min.**

Ingredients:

Ginger, fresh, peeled,
  thinly sliced   125 gm
Salt   ½ tsp / 3 gm
Vinegar   8½ tbsp / 125 ml
Castor sugar   1 tbsp / 15 gm

Method:

1. Soak the ginger in a bowl of cold water for 30 minutes.
2. Boil a saucepan of water and add the ginger without the water in which it was soaked. Boil again on high heat, drain and keep aside to cool.
3. Place the ginger on a plate and sprinkle the salt.
4. In a saucepan, add the vinegar and sugar and heat till the sugar dissolves completely.
5. Place the ginger in a jar and pour the mixture over it. Mix thoroughly and let it to cool. Then cover and refrigerate.
6. The pickled ginger will turn a pale pink colour and will be ready for consumption after 1 week. It can be stored in the refrigerator for 3-4 months.

Nam Khao Dong
Rice water pickle

Ingredients:

Water	12 cups / 2.4 lt
Rice	250 gm
Radish, peeled, thinly sliced	1
Carrots, peeled, thinly sliced	2
Cabbage, thinly sliced	375 gm
Garlic cloves, thinly sliced	3
Ginger, fresh, peeled, thinly sliced	1 tbsp / 15 gm
Black peppercorns	1 tsp / 5 gm
Salt	2 tbsp / 30 gm
Shallots, peeled	1
Red chillies, large, fresh	2

Method:

1. In a large saucepan, bring the water to a boil. Add the rice and boil for 15 minutes.
2. Strain the water off the rice into a bowl, keep aside and let it cool. Discard the rice.
3. Layer the vegetables in a big jar, with garlic, black peppercorns and salt between each layer. Top with salt. Bury the shallots and red chillies in the middle.
4. Add the cooled rice water just enough to cover the top layer. Cover with a muslin cloth and keep aside for 4 days in a cool place. If the level of the liquid drops then add some more cold water.
5. After 4 days the pickle will be ready for consumption. The pickle will stay for several weeks if stored in an airtight jar and refrigerated.

Suggested Menus

Soups and Starters
Tom Yam Koong   10
(*Traditional Thai soup with prawns*)
Satay Kai (*Marinated chicken on sticks*)   24

Main Course
Hor Mok Thalay   38
(*Seafood baked in coconut shell*)
Gang Keyo Wun Gai   49
(*Chicken in green curry*)

Accompaniments
Khao Phad Phak (*Vegetable fried rice*)   68
Baa Mee Phad Thalay   82
(*Stir-fried noodles with seafood*)

Soups and Starters
Tom Kha Kai   16
(*Chicken and ginger soup*)
Som Tum (*Raw papaya salad*)   32

Main Course
Gung Pad Kratien   40
(*Stir-fried prawns with garlic*)
Patani (*Stir-fried lamb*)   54

Accompaniments
Khao Phad Bai Krapaw Kai   70
(*Chicken fried rice*)
Guey Tiew Phat Khee Mao   76
(*Stir-fried noodles*)

Glossary of Cooking Terms

Blanch — Immerse in boiling water so that the peel comes off.

Deep-fry — Fry food in fat or oil sufficient to cover it.

Poach — Cook (fish, etc) by simmering in a small amount of liquid.

Sauté — Fry quickly over strong heat in fat or oil.

Simmer — Keep boiling gently on low heat.

Skewer — Fasten together pieces of food compactly on a specially designed long pin, for cooking.

Stir-fry — Fry rapidly while stirring and tossing.

Stock — Liquid produced when meat, poultry, bones, vegetables are simmered in water with herbs and flavouring for several hours; stock forms the basis of soups, stews, etc.

Index

ACCOMPANIMENTS

Rice

Noodles

Sauces

Pickles

ISBN: 81-7436-126-X

Third impression 2004
© **Roli & Janssen BV 2000**
Published in India by Roli Books
in arrangement with Roli & Janssen
M-75 Greater Kailash II (Market)
New Delhi 110 048, India
Ph: ++91 (011) 29212271, 29212782, 29210886
Fax: ++91 (011) 29217185, E-mail: roli@vsnl.com
Website: rolibooks.com

Photographs: Dheeraj Paul

Printed and bound in Singapore